YOU CALL THAT A
FARM?

Raising Otters, Leeches, Weeds,

and Other Unusual Things

SAM AND BERYL EPSTEIN

FARRAR · STRAUS · GIROUX
New York

Text copyright © 1991 by Sam and Beryl Epstein
All rights reserved
Published simultaneously in Canada by HarperCollins*CanadaLtd*
Printed in the United States of America
First edition, 1991

Library of Congress Cataloging-in-Publication Data
Epstein, Sam.
  You call that a farm? : raising otters, leeches, weeds,
and other unusual things / Sam and Beryl Epstein. — 1st ed.
    p.   cm.
  Summary: Describes the activities at several farms where
unusual plants or animals are raised.
  1. Animal culture—Juvenile literature. 2. Farms—Juvenile
literature. 3. Hay-fever plants—Juvenile literature.
[1. Farms.] I. Epstein, Beryl Williams. II. Title.
SF75.5.E67 1991 636—dc20   90-56157   CIP AC

Contents

Why We Wrote This Book

One day we saw a story in the news about a man who raises leeches. Of course, we wondered why anyone would want anything to do with these slimy creatures. So we read the story and soon found out. And we were fascinated. We put the story in our folder marked *Ideas*, where we keep clippings that might someday give us an idea for a book.

We knew we'd probably never write a book about leeches. But we know that if we think about one thing for a while, it sometimes leads us to thinking about something else. And then that something else may give us an idea for a book we'd like to write.

Not long afterward, we read another fascinating newspaper story. This one was about a family that raises weeds, and in it we learned that weeds can be a very valuable crop. We put that one in the *Ideas* folder, too.

From then on, we kept adding to our folder other stories about raising surprising things—such as alligators and parrots, for example—which we'd never before thought that people actually raised, the way farmers raise cows or chickens. And after a while we began to think of all these stories as stories about farms—unusual farms, that is. Finally, we realized we'd like to write a book about such places.

We got in touch with people who owned some of the farms, and asked if we could visit them and find out what it's like to do what they do. And we told them why we wanted that information.

"We think young people would like to know about your farms," we said. "Then they might even think of some unusual crop they'd raise themselves someday."

All the farmers of unusual things we talked to said they'd be glad to help us. And they did. We were able to find out about their farms, and we wrote this book so you can learn about them, too.

OTTERS

Bringing Them Back

It was a perfectly ordinary February morning at the Sevin house in the small Louisiana town of Theriot. A bright sun swelled the buds on the trees outside and warmed the sluggish water of the bayou flowing past the yard.

Diane Sevin was in the kitchen, with the month-old otter she was about to feed. Tom Sevin, her son, was on the screened porch preparing the food he would soon carry out to dozens of cages of adult otters. Lee Roy Sevin, Diane's husband, was answering a telephone call from a man eager to buy a pair of otters for his zoo thousands of miles away.

Then the Sevins' two-year-old granddaughter, Lee Ann, holding her mother's hand, came into the kitchen from her home next door. Today, for the first time, she was going to be allowed to come close to one of the young otters on her grandparents' otter farm. These otter pups are hand-fed, so they become accustomed to people and can be sold to zoos or as pets.

Diane Sevin sat down, cradling the little towel-wrapped otter in one arm. The liquid formula she had mixed for it was in a warmed baby bottle. Her husband finished his call and joined her. Tom Sevin came in from the porch. Lee Ann's mother stood just behind her.

"Don't touch him," Diane told the little girl softly, as she put the bottle's nipple into the cub's mouth.

Lee Roy Sevin knelt beside her. "You've got to talk to them," he whispered to Lee Ann. Then, in his soft voice, he spoke to the little otter. "C'mon, baby," he said. "Let's eat now, you little boogalee."

There was a faint sucking noise. The otter was taking his food.

Lee Ann watched closely. "Baby!" she whispered after a moment. She was smiling delightedly.

The grownups around her smiled, too. They knew that living next door to the Sevins' Bayou Otter Farm could be hard for a little girl if she didn't like otters. But now they felt pretty sure they wouldn't have to worry about Lee Ann.

"She calls all the little ones 'my babies' now," Diane Sevin said a few days later.

Most people like otters the moment they see them. An otter's big eyes and handsome flaring whiskers make its broad face seem almost human. It moves and plays in endearing ways—slithering smoothly through water, humping rather awkwardly over land, sliding boisterously down a mud bank into a stream, and then climbing back up to take another slide. And when an otter catches a fish with its swift-moving front paws, it holds its squirming meal firmly between its paws and bites into it like a greedy child.

Otters were plentiful all over North America when Lee Roy's and Diane's French ancestors first came to this continent, to settle in a Canadian colony called Acadia. The Acadians, as the new colonists came to be called, learned that otters' soft dark pelts brought high prices from fur dealers, and many Acadians became skilled otter trappers.

Other colonists, and Native Americans as well, were also trapping vast numbers of otters for their skins. At the same time, otters were losing their living space to people who were building towns along rivers and streams. Otters became more and more scarce. Finally, the only place in North America where they were still plentiful was the wild

Lee Roy Sevin's otter pups learn early that humans can be friendly

© 1990 BY DENVER A. BRYAN

southernmost region of Louisiana. That low, flat land, crisscrossed by creeks and small rivers called bayous, was still a safe home for otters.

Lee Roy's and Diane's families had been among the many Acadians who moved to Louisiana from Canada. Their Louisiana neighbors pronounced "Acadian" as "Cajun," which soon became the name used by the settlers from Canada.

Cajuns continued to earn their living as their forefathers had, by hunting, fishing, and trapping, and they went on using their own language. A barefoot Lee Roy Sevin learned the skills his father had learned from his own father, and spoke nothing but French.

Diane was in Lee Roy's class on their first day of school. They still remember how frightened they were when they learned that English was the only language permitted in their classroom.

"And we didn't know a word of English!" Diane says.

They learned English, of course. They had to. And when they grew up and married, their own children learned English at home. By then, Lee Roy was working for a company that bought and sold bayou land and planned its development for conservation purposes and such industries as fish canneries and oil refineries. He also became a state official in charge of issuing licenses to hunters and trappers, and to dealers in animal skins. He still trapped otters himself, because their skins brought in the extra money his family needed.

But, even as a boy, Lee Roy Sevin had never enjoyed killing an otter. He had a special feeling for the big-eyed creatures. It seemed quite natural to him to use the Cajun pet name, boogalee, for both a small otter and a small child.

So he was delighted one day when he got a call from a curator of a zoo in Missouri, where there were no longer any wild otters. The curator offered to pay him $100 for a live otter, to be shown to Missourians who had never seen one.

The price alone amazed Sevin. It was more than double what he received for the finest otter skin. He agreed readily to the sale. But the call had pleased him for a totally different reason. It gave him the chance to save one otter's life. And as soon as he'd delivered a fine healthy otter to the Missouri zoo, he was asking himself if other zoos might be interested in a similar purchase.

To find the answer to his question, he put a small ad in a magazine for animal-lovers—a magazine zoo curators were likely to read. He and Diane could scarcely believe what happened when the magazine reached its readers.

"I got more letters than I could answer!" Sevin says. "They poured in!" The letters came not only from zoos but from owners of animal parks and from people who simply wanted an otter as a pet.

The Sevins began planning a way to give at least some of those letter writers what they wanted, and to save the lives of many otters at the same time. In the winter of that year, 1957, they started their Bayou Otter Farm.

They couldn't afford to waste time. The annual two-month otter-trapping season would soon begin. As a first step, Sevin got in touch with trappers licensed to catch otters that year. He told them he would pay more for live otters, if they were healthy and unharmed, than the trappers could get for the pelts.

To make sure the otters were unharmed, he wanted a change in the leg-hold trap required by law. That trap caught the animal by the leg or the foot and did little damage to its pelt. Sevin wanted the trappers to use a trap that caught the animal by one or two toes and did not even break its skin. He also asked the trappers to visit their traps early every morning, and often during the day. If they did that, no animal would be in the trap for long and they would suffer as little as possible.

Sevin built sturdy wire-and-wood cages for the otters that were soon being brought to him. He expected to be feeding them for some time, since most people wanted the otters delivered in the spring or early summer.

At first, the Sevins fed the otters the same fish otters catch for themselves in the bayous. That didn't seem completely satisfactory for caged otters, so the Sevins tried meat instead. That proved no better. Otters obviously needed many of the same things human beings need, such as vitamins and fiber, as well as protein. So, through trial and error, the Sevins developed the mixed diet their otters are now fed twice each day.

Tom Sevin with the Sevin family's pet otter, named Rascal. Rascal is soft and cuddly and playful, but he is also surprisingly strong. "If he wanted to get away from me, I couldn't hold him," Tom says

PHOTO BY SAM EPSTEIN

Among the things that go into that diet are skinned and cleaned nutria, the large rat-like creatures found in every bayou. To the nutria Tom Sevin usually adds fish, cereal, a commercial chick feed, lemons, and cod-liver oil. Occasionally, there are eggs in the mixture, too. The meat is first put through a grinder, and then everything is mixed in a concrete mixer—the only machine the Sevins could find that was big enough for their purpose.

Very young otters get their own special food, even after Diane stops feeding them by bottle. Their vegetables are chopped up in a blender. Their meat is carefully chosen. The Sevins can remember buying veal for their young otters and then using the trimmings from the expensive meat for their own dinner.

The Sevins' otter pups are born on the farm to female otters trapped before they gave birth. Because of the personal care the Sevins give the pups, they grow up to feel friendly toward people, who will keep them as pets or come to see them in zoos.

Even visitors to the farm who are allowed to see the pups may not enter the broad grassy aisles between the rows of adult otters' cages. Lee Roy Sevin has these cages high above the ground, on wooden supports. Only he and Tom approach them, and they do so as little as possible.

There is good reason for isolating these animals from the public. These are otters which will be delivered by spring or early summer to the Wildlife Departments of states whose native otter population long ago disappeared. The Sevins' largest annual order of otters is now delivered to the state of Missouri, whose zoo once bought its first single otter from Lee Roy Sevin. In one recent year, Missouri received four hundred otters from the Bayou Otter Farm.

Each year, on certain days announced ahead of time to the public, trucks from the Sevins' otter farm arrive at a Missouri riverbank. The cages from the trucks are carried to the water's edge and one by one they are opened and the otters are released.

The animals ignore the people who have gathered to watch them.

An otter taking its first step to freedom pays no attention to its fascinated audience

If they had spent a lot of time with people, they might remain on the shore, waiting to be fed. But because they have been kept away from human beings as much as possible, they are ready to live once more the life in the wild which they had known before their capture.

"We have to make sure that the otters going back to the wild haven't learned to stay close to people—to depend on people," Lee Roy Sevin says. "That's the only way they'll be able to take care of themselves when they're once more where they belong."

He is likely to make that point whenever he meets with people interested in returning otters to areas where otters lived long ago. And if he and Diane happen to be at a European scientific conference, he can say it just as clearly in the French he and Diane have not forgotten.

Most visitors to the Bayou Otter Farm agree with what Lee Roy Sevin says. They probably also agree that any otter which spends part of its life in captivity is very lucky indeed if it spends that time with the Sevins.

MYSID SHRIMP

Testing for Poisonous Garbage

Anybody might wonder why Robert Valenti raises the little sea creatures called mysid (pronounced "my-sid") shrimp. They're almost colorless, and scarcely half an inch long, so nobody wants them in an aquarium with brilliant tropical fish. They're not useful as food, so he can't sell them to fish shops or restaurants.

Robert Valenti, a scientist himself, knows that certain government scientists need mysid shrimp, and he knows why. Those scientists use them to test the tons of garbage that are loaded onto barges every year and carried down rivers to be dumped into the sea. The tiny shrimp let the scientists know whether or not a bargeload of garbage could poison the ocean and the fish that live in it, and endanger the lives of people who eat seafood or who swim at ocean beaches.

Robert Valenti has spent years studying and raising fish and shellfish in and near New York. He has grown striped bass, for example, in the big outdoor tanks he built on the shore of Napeague Bay, near the eastern tip of Long Island. In those tanks, and the row of low buildings alongside them, he operates the business he calls Multi Aquaculture Systems. Its name tells people that he raises a variety of creatures—mysid shrimp are among them—that live in water. His wife and partner, Marie, and their assistants are all trained scientists, too.

The floor of their crowded office, in one of the buildings, is damp and sandy from the boots that everyone on the staff wears, indoors and out. The single big chair in the room is usually occupied by a very large old dog. A second large dog sleeps on a mattress in the corner. One frequent visitor is a neighbor's rooster, which slips through the door if it is left open and tries to steal some of the dogs' food. The dogs growl and snap at him and the rooster fights back with its sharp spurs. There may be a wild duck with an injured wing waddling around the office for weeks, until it is well enough to fly off.

The tanks Valenti's shrimp will live in are lined up on sturdy tables in another low building. The tanks are filled with water that has been taken from the bay and left for a few days in a covered container. By the end of that time, any bacteria in the water that could be harmful to mysid shrimp are dead and harmless. They have starved to death after eating up everything in the water that could serve them as food. But the microscopic plants in the water, called algae, have formed a greenish scum, or bloom, which mysid shrimp can safely eat. Finally, air is pumped into the water to supply the oxygen the shrimp need. Now the tanks are ready to be safe homes for these tiny creatures, and the shrimp can be put into them.

Part of the water in each tank will be removed every month and replaced by freshly treated water in which harmful bacteria have already starved to death. And air must be pumped into every tank that has shrimp in it. Without the constant supply of oxygen which the air puts into the water, the shrimp would be dead within an hour.

One evening, when Valenti and his staff were finishing the day's work, a car crashed into the power-line pole on the road at the edge of his property. The crash cut off the power running his air pumps. Valenti immediately started his electric generator. And all night long he and his staff worked steadily, shifting the emergency power from one place to another, so the supply of oxygen to the shrimp tanks was never cut off for more than a few minutes. It didn't occur to any of

Robert and Marie Valenti in their working clothes

them to leave. And the next morning, when the power line was repaired, the shrimp were alive and well.

Except for a rare emergency of that sort, the work at Valenti's shrimp farm, as people often speak of it, seems pretty simple. In what Valenti calls the communal tank, both male and female mysid shrimp swim about, mate, and produce their young. The young are born still attached to the yellowish yolk which surrounded the tiny bodies before birth. This yolk becomes their first food.

Every Monday, Valenti empties into the communal tank a meal of special shrimp food—thousands of dried eggs of another small shrimp, called brine shrimp. These eggs are inside hard, dry cases called cysts. Within forty-eight hours, those cysts, and the eggs inside them, soften in the water. The cysts open. The eggs hatch into newborn shrimp, called nauplii. As the empty cysts float up to the surface, the water in the tank swarms with the nauplii.

A mysid shrimp uses the front pair of its six pairs of legs to gather up quantities of this food. It stuffs the nauplii into the pouch beneath

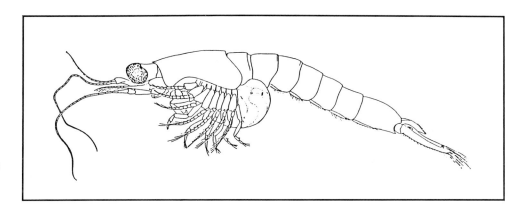

This drawing of a mysid shrimp is about fourteen times the shrimp's actual size

its mouth. When the pouch is full, the mysid can swim about at leisure, tearing food out of its storage place, a bit at a time, until the pouch needs refilling.

Mysid shrimp reach their full growth at the end of a week. And female mysid may give birth more than once a week for the three months they live. Both male and female require nothing more from Valenti than their regular oxygen supply, a monthly replacement of tank water, and that one feeding each week.

But raising mysid shrimp for the scientists who need them is not as simple as it looks, because the shrimp are useful to scientists for only five days after they are born. After that, the shrimp may not be sensitive enough to detect dangerous substances. So, when Valenti receives a scientist's order—it may be for several hundred or several thousand—he must be able to ship shrimp that have just been born. To make sure those orders can be filled, he uses a small net to pick out of the communal tank a number of females that are about to give birth. He can recognize them because there is a swelling at the front of their bodies. He puts them in their own special tank and will remove their offspring from that tank within hours after they are born.

Only a very sharp eye can see a thread-like newborn mysid shrimp. And it can be safely picked up only with an eyedropper. This is how Steve Johndrew of Valenti's staff carries out that delicate job.

First he moves some of the water in the tank, along with the shrimp it contains, to a flat glass dish. A light under the dish makes it easier to see the shrimp. He squeezes the bulb of the eyedropper, to force the air out of it, and then lowers the tip of the dropper into the dish. When it is close to a shrimp, he releases the bulb. This sucks both water and shrimp into the glass tube. Sometimes two or three or even four shrimp are sucked into the tube at once.

Then he moves the eyedropper to the mouth of a plastic bottle half filled with the kind of treated water used in the shrimp tanks. He lowers the open end of the tube into the water and gently squeezes the bulb.

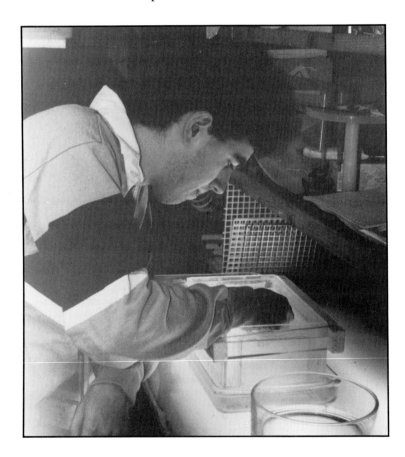

Steve Johndrew uses an eyedropper to pick up day-old mysid shrimp for a shipment

PHOTO BY SAM EPSTEIN

The water in the tube, along with the shrimp, is forced into the bottle. Steve Johndrew can transfer a couple of hundred shrimp from the dish to the bottle in about fifteen minutes.

The tiny shrimp are now in the container in which they will be shipped. Each of the gallon bottles Johndrew uses can safely hold a thousand shrimp. Then pure oxygen is pumped into it, and the bottle is sealed shut and enclosed in a sturdy carton. It is ready for the air-express truck driver who calls at Marie Valenti's office every day.

The government scientist who receives the package makes use of the shrimp immediately. He puts mysid shrimp into bowls of water containing samples from a load of garbage. If the shrimp swim energetically about in a series of such tests, the garbage-laden barge is permitted to go on its way out to sea.

But the shrimp may die. Or they may behave in strange ways, such as swimming in circles, or upside down. If either of these things happens, the scientist knows the garbage contains dangerous chemicals, metals, or disease-causing germs. That kind of garbage can kill thousands of fish and shellfish, or contaminate them so that people who eat them will get sick and perhaps die. It can also pollute the water along beaches and make them unsafe for swimmers.

So, if the shrimp die or behave strangely, the scientist gives orders that this load of garbage must be handled in a special way. The barge may be ordered to scatter its load over many miles of water, to prevent a large amount of it from settling in any one place. This will reduce the damage it can cause to sea life.

Robert Valenti's mysid shrimp can't protect the sea from the harm done by the thousands of tons of garbage dumped into it every year. But, until a better solution to the world's vast waste problem is found, the little shrimp can help guard against some of the worst effects of garbage. And that, Robert Valenti believes, is reason enough for raising these tiny creatures that must be handled so carefully during the brief time they live in the tanks of his shrimp farm.

LEECHES

Once Again, Used by Doctors

"Yuck! Slimy little bloodsuckers!"

That's the sort of thing a lot of people say when they hear the word "leeches." And though some leeches eat worms or other small forms of life, it's true that most leeches are exactly what so many people call them. They are slimy and they are bloodsuckers, living on the blood they suck from other living creatures.

But when young Roy Sawyer saw a leech stuck to his leg as he waded in a marsh close to his home near Charleston, South Carolina, he was likely to say, "Great! Another one!" He went wading, in fact, in the hope that he'd pick up leeches that way for his collection. The boy who would someday start the world's first leech farm already thought the slimy bloodsuckers were fascinating.

When Roy was fourteen years old, he wrote a report on his collection of leeches for his high-school science class. Some of the leeches he described were unknown to scientists at the time, probably because very few scientists had any interest in leeches.

Of course, it was well known that leeches had been used for hundreds of years as a kind of medicine. Doctors thought diseases were caused by what they called "bad blood," and put leeches on their patients to suck that blood out. The treatment was called "bleeding." If a man had a stomachache, for example, his doctor might put leeches on his stomach, sometimes as many as fifty at once. If a patient had a toothache, the leeches were put inside his mouth, with a thread tied to each one, so it could be pulled back if the patient accidentally swallowed it.

When one of the major causes of disease was found to be the tiny forms of life called microbes, however, doctors turned to the new microbe-killing medicines. From then on, "bleeding" was very seldom used.

Roy Sawyer was still interested in leeches when he went to the University of Michigan, but he hadn't yet met anyone who was as enthusiastic about them as he was. Then he read about Professor E. W. Knight-Jones, a world authority on leeches. To become his student, Roy left the United States for Wales, in the British Isles. At the University of Wales, in Swansea, Roy studied marine, or saltwater, leeches and earned his doctorate. Swansea proved a very satisfactory place for him. He had no trouble collecting as many leeches as he needed for his work, by wading in the nearby marshes. He married Lorna, the Welsh girl he fell in love with. And she didn't complain when she sometimes had to change her party shoes for boots after a dance, so they could hunt leeches on the way home.

After a time, supported by Lorna's salary as a teacher, Dr. Sawyer began writing the huge three-volume book that would make him known as one of the world's experts on leeches. In it, he would describe the more than six hundred varieties of leeches that are known in the world, ranging in size from a few inches to eighteen inches long. One of the best-known was the medicinal leech, so called because it was the one that doctors had once used. The largest, as Dr. Sawyer learned from an old French publication, was the rare and little-known giant Amazon, which sucked up its food through a long, pointed tube called a proboscis. And the Amazon, instead of living for only two to six years, as smaller leeches do, had been said to live as long as twenty years.

Dr. Sawyer's growing reputation soon brought him an invitation that took Lorna and himself to the University of California in Berkeley. An important scientist there, Gunther Stent, wanted Dr. Sawyer to set up a project that would make use of embryo leeches—leeches not yet hatched. Professor Stent believed that their very simple bodies could help scientists to understand the nervous system of our more complicated human bodies.

At Berkeley, Dr. Sawyer had a variety of leeches to work with, but there were no Amazons among them, and he had grown very curious about the largest of all leeches. So he managed to have two of them

Dr. Roy Sawyer holding one of his giant Amazon leeches
PHOTO BY JONATHAN PLAYER
NEW YORK TIMES PICTURES

sent to him from South America. One died soon after it arrived at the Berkeley laboratory and Dr. Sawyer feared that the other would soon die, too, along with the offspring it had produced. He decided he didn't know enough about the food and water temperature Amazons required if they were to stay healthy in a laboratory, so he organized and led a scientific expedition to the part of South America where the Amazon leeches had been hatched.

There, wading through a tropical swamp, he snatched up out of the water the first Amazon he ever caught. And when the scientists returned to Berkeley they knew how to keep their new specimens alive and healthy. By the time Roy and Lorna were ready to leave California, thirty-five of the giant leeches were flourishing in the Berkeley laboratory.

He took some of the Amazons back to Wales and began to breed them, while continuing his studies of other leeches, too. Everything he learned about the bloodsuckers, large and small, went into the big book he was working on.

One of the things he learned from his research was that the saliva in the mouths of medicinal leeches contains an anesthetic, or painkiller. This explained why he'd never felt any pain when he'd been bitten by leeches as a boy, back in South Carolina. Their painkilling saliva had spread over his skin before their tiny teeth pierced it.

Another substance in their saliva interested him, too. Something in that saliva appeared to keep blood from coagulating—from forming the thick jelly-like clots that often stop the flow of blood shortly after it has started. Any substance that prevents that flow is called an anticoagulant. The anticoagulant in the medicinal leech's saliva has been given the name hirudin.

These substances, Dr. Sawyer realized, were useful to a leech in its search for food. He began to wonder if they might not also be useful to human beings.

Then he discovered that the saliva of the Amazon had a special substance in it, too. Like the hirudin in the medicinal leech, it could prevent the clotting of blood—but it could do more than that. This substance, called hementin, could dissolve blood clots after they had formed.

For Dr. Sawyer, hementin was an amazing discovery. For one thing, he thought scientists might make use of it in the future to save the lives of people who had heart attacks caused by blood clots. For another, it indicated that not all leeches have the same substances in their bodies. This meant it might be possible to find very different substances—even more remarkable ones perhaps than had already been found—in leech saliva.

He decided he would have to start raising his own leeches—hundreds of leeches, of many different kinds. He would have to start a leech farm. And with the support of Lorna and her family, and a grant from the government, that's what he did.

Dr. Sawyer didn't look for a fertile piece of land for the farm he planned to establish in Swansea, Wales. He needed a building. First he rented what had once been a steel mill. Later he transferred his farm to a big Victorian mansion he bought and remodeled for his special purposes.

There is plenty of space in the house and its adjoining buildings for his leech tanks. Each tank has a tightly fastened cloth cover to keep the leeches from getting out, as they will do if they have the chance.

In some rooms, the air is kept warm and the water in the tanks is warm, too. These are breeding tanks, where leeches lay their eggs inside soft bag-like cocoons that their bodies produce. The leeches also hatch in these tanks. In other rooms, both air and water are cool. This keeps leeches sluggish and slow-moving, so they're easy to remove from the tanks for study.

The food Dr. Sawyer gives his leeches is, of course, blood—cow blood bought from the local cattle-slaughtering house. It is in sausage-shaped bags made of pigs' intestines, which are hung in the tanks. Leeches bite into the bags, suck up blood for fifteen or twenty minutes, until they are full, and then drop off.

The Victorian mansion named Bryngelen House, with its new one-story addition called Ty Gelen, now houses Biopharm's Wales headquarters offices, a lecture hall, and the warm and cool rooms in which thousands of leeches are raised every year

PHOTO COURTESY
BIOPHARM LTD

For the first three months after they are born, leeches are fed once a month. As adults they eat less often. When adult leeches have their fill of blood, they are not hungry again for months, perhaps even for a year. And since a leech won't eat unless it is hungry, Dr. Sawyer feeds his leeches on a careful schedule, so that some tanks are always full of the hungry leeches he might need for experiments.

Those experiments, which Dr. Sawyer and his staff still carry out in the farm's laboratories, soon aroused the interest of the manufacturers of today's medicines. Some of them came to believe, as Dr. Sawyer did, that leeches might be the source of new and important medicines. They asked him for material to help with their own research, and he sent samples of the saliva his assistants "milked," a drop at a time, from the mouths of certain leeches.

Amazon leeches couldn't be "milked" at all, because of their long, sucking tubes, so a new method had to be devised for working with them. Almost everything that goes on at the leech farm seems to demand methods never tried before. And the big Amazons, natives of tropical marshes, require special care to keep them alive and well.

When the farm was a year old, its tanks held five thousand leeches. Dr. Sawyer wished he could afford many more.

Then one night, when he was not home, Lorna had a telephone call from the other side of the Atlantic Ocean. Dr. Joseph Upton, a micro-surgeon—a surgeon whose operations are performed under a micro-scope—was calling from the Boston Children's Hospital. He asked if a few dozen leeches could be sent to him immediately, and explained why he wanted them.

One of his patients, he told Lorna, was a five-year-old boy named Guy whose ear had been bitten off by a dog. Guy's mother had rushed her son, and his ear, to the hospital. The operation Dr. Upton had performed, to sew the ear back on, had required him to repair torn arteries and veins.

The arteries, which are larger than veins, hadn't given him too much trouble. And once they were mended, blood had begun to flow again from the boy's heart. But working on the hair-sized veins through which the blood had to return to the heart had been more difficult. After ten hours of work under a powerful microscope, he had been able to repair only four of them.

Still, his operation had seemed successful. But then the ear had turned blue and had started to swell. Next it turned purple and the swelling increased. This meant that the very tiny veins had become clogged, halting the flow of blood between heart and ear. Unless the flow could be restored, Guy's ear could not be saved; it would have to be cut off.

Dr. Upton had remembered something he had learned as an army surgeon during the war in Vietnam. Medical leeches were still in use there, and Dr. Upton had used them to keep patients' blood flowing freely during operations. So, in the hope that they could help Guy, he had tried to find a source of leeches somewhere in the United States.

His efforts had been completely unsuccessful, but then someone had told him about Dr. Sawyer, who raised leeches in Wales.

The moment Dr. Upton finished his story, Lorna Sawyer assured him that the leeches he wanted would be put aboard the next jet plane leaving for Boston.

Immediately after she hung up, she packed about thirty leeches in a waterproof container, along with wet moss to keep them moist. Then she put the container in a sturdy box and drove three hours to the London airport to get the box on a plane for Boston.

Dr. Upton was at the Boston airport when the plane arrived. He rushed the leeches to the hospital and put two of the hungry creatures on Guy's ear. They began to suck up blood at once.

"The ear perked up right away," Dr. Upton said later. "It was obvious it was going to work."

The first pair of leeches became full and dropped off. New hungry pairs replaced them, one after the other. By the end of a week, blood was flowing steadily between the ear and the heart, giving the torn veins a chance to heal. Guy's ear had been saved.

Newspapers reported the story. Guy was suddenly famous, and so was the man who had bred the leeches that had come from Wales.

Almost overnight, it seemed, microsurgeons on every continent wanted leeches for their patients. By 1988, when the farm was four years old, Dr. Sawyer was shipping out a hundred thousand leeches a year. More than half of them went to his home town, Charleston. He had set up a center there for distributing leeches to American doctors and to hospitals that had decided to keep supplies of them on hand.

The center's director, Lynn Hills, had grown up in South Carolina, as Dr. Sawyer did, but until she joined his staff she'd felt the way most people feel about leeches. Now she says, "They're fascinating!"

When she gets word from Wales that a shipment is on the way, she makes sure she has enough tanks for them and that the water in the tanks is clean and the right temperature. Opening boxes containing hundreds of leeches, and transferring the wriggling creatures to new homes, is a delicate business, but she has become an expert at it. When it's time to ship them out again, she uses a small net to scoop the right number of leeches into a bag, along with wet moss. She then seals the bag and packs it in Styrofoam to keep the leeches cool.

The growing sales of live leeches give Dr. Sawyer more funds for his own experiments, and allow other scientists and industries to experiment with leeches, too.

He calls his farm Biopharm. "Bio," the first part of the name, is the Greek word for "life." The second part—which sounds just like "farm," of course—is from another Greek word that means "giving drugs or medicines." And a biopharm, Dr. Sawyer believes, is just what leeches will prove to be: a living pharmacy, a drugstore offering new medicines made possible by those slimy bloodsuckers that have fascinated him all his life.

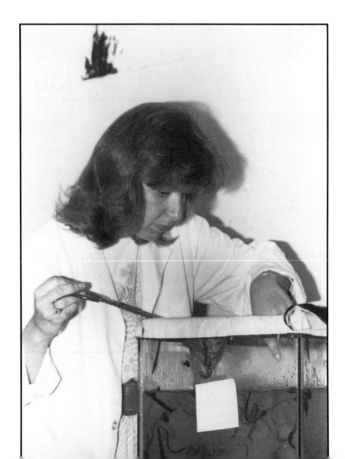

Lynn Hills scooping up leeches for shipment to a hospital
PHOTO BY SAM EPSTEIN

PARROTS

Pampered Birds for Zoos and Pets

Cheryl Forker and her husband, Daryl, once had thirteen pet parrots in their house in Miami, Florida. Neighbors complained about the parrots' constant squeals and howls and screams and chatter. They said the Forkers should be ordered to remove the birds from their property.

The Forkers responded by removing both themselves and the birds. They bought several acres of land outside of town, and several more parrots, and started a parrot farm. The Feather Connection, as they call it, now raises hundreds of birds every year.

Like any farm, it demands its owners' attention seven days a week. Daryl Forker is the manager and the Forkers have several trained assistants. Their daughter is in charge of the farm's nursery, where all parrot chicks are kept for two or three weeks after they are born. This accustoms them to being handled by human beings, and will make them friendly pets. Cheryl Forker herself, whose knowledge of parrots has earned the farm its worldwide reputation, still works long hours every day with the birds. She even seems pleased when it is sometimes necessary for her to replace her daughter in the nursery.

Feeding the chicks—there may be as many as a hundred in the

room—begins at nine o'clock in the morning. They are all fed every three hours, and the last feeding isn't finished until one o'clock the next morning.

Each chick has its own bed, an ordinary plastic box of the kind usually used for storing leftovers in a refrigerator. The open boxes stand in rows on shelves along one wall of the nursery, where the temperature is kept at 93°F. The smallest birds lie in boxes so small they can be lined with an ordinary facecloth. Boxes for larger birds are lined with face towels or bath towels, each folded in a special way. All the towels and cloths are changed after every feeding, so the Forker laundry room is always busy.

Cheryl follows the same schedule in the nursery that she taught her daughter. Wearing a pair of sterile, or germ-free, rubber gloves, she prepares the food for the first chick.

Each variety of young parrot has its own formula, and it is much like the food its mother might give it. A mother parrot eats several kinds of foods, and swallows them down into her crop, a sort of pocket in a bird's throat. There the foods are partly digested and mixed with the mother's warm saliva. Then she regurgitates the food—she brings it back up into her beak. And from her beak she pokes it into the chick's throat.

For the first chick of the day, Cheryl may make a mixture of several soft, mushed-up foods. These may include corn, oatmeal, sweet potato, applesauce, and banana. Or she may use a mixture sent to her by a manufacturer for whom she tests new varieties of parrot-chick food. She thins the mixture with sterile water from a special faucet in the room; the water from that faucet has been heated to exactly 103°F.

After she has lifted the chick out of its box, Cheryl first cleans its mouth with a cotton swab that is on the end of a small stick. Then she chooses a sterile syringe of the right size for the chick's beak. Holding the chick's beak open with one hand, she fills the syringe with the formula and lets one drop of the liquid fall onto her wrist, like a human mother testing the milk in her baby's bottle to make sure it is not too warm or too cool. When she is satisfied, she squeezes the formula out of the syringe, bit by bit, into the chick's throat. Soon the throat's loose skin swells into a bulge as the food settles into the chick's crop. Eventually, the food will move on down into its stomach.

When the crop is full, or the chick refuses to eat any more, Cheryl puts the syringe into a sterilizer, where it will remain for several hours before it can be used again. Then she picks up a soft cloth and cleans the chick. She carefully wipes the soft fuzz that will soon be replaced by real feathers. She cleans between the toes of the tiny feet and around the slender metal band on one leg. On that band are her initials and the number of her license to breed and sell parrots. This chick, like all her other birds, has its own record in her files. On it are the date of the bird's birth and the names of its parents.

Cheryl Forker uses a syringe to feed a parrot chick

PHOTO BY SAM EPSTEIN

Finally, Cheryl returns the young parrot to its freshly lined box. She throws away the gloves she has been wearing, puts on a fresh sterile pair, and starts to prepare the food for the next chick.

There are several big cages in the nursery, too. They hold colorful birds a foot tall or more. Although the birds seem to be full grown, they are all less than three months old. They belong to special breeds that are hand-fed until they reach the age of three months and can then be sold.

Sometimes one of the caged birds already has a new owner, who may have paid as much as $10,000 for it. Some new owners visit their birds regularly. Every visit helps the bird buyer and the parrot to become acquainted and learn each other's ways. One new owner brought her bird a small plush animal to keep in its cage. When the bird left the nursery, she told Cheryl, the toy animal would go with it. It would be a comforting link, she said, between its first home in the nursery and its new one with her.

Cheryl welcomes these visits. They help her show customers the kind of care and respect she gives her birds, which she expects their new owners to give them, too.

The busiest room in the Forker house, after the nursery, is the kitchen. There, two patient men prepare the food needed for the four hundred or more adult parrots usually living on the Forker farm. The birds are fed three times a day, and each kind has its own diet.

The men make corn bread every morning, and a sweet cake that will be given to some birds as a special treat. They spend hours preparing the parrots' meals from the supplies kept in an outdoor shed. The shed's largest coolers hold corn on the cob, carrots, and apples. There are boxes of mangoes, celery, and grapes, and others filled with coconut meat, Brazil nuts, walnuts, and almonds. Bunches of green papayas and green bananas hang from wires, slowly ripening. Sunflower seeds are stored in large quantities, until they sprout; these sprouts are an important fresh food for the birds.

There are two large parrots that live inside the house. Sometimes

Cheryl Forker visits the cage of a white cockatoo that was one of her original thirteen pets

PHOTO BY SAM EPSTEIN

perched on the back of a chair, sometimes flying about, they are often in or near the kitchen. "Merry Christmas!" one calls out, when somebody passes by. A couple of the Forker dogs wander in and out of the kitchen, too. The birds may scream at the dogs, and the dogs may bark at the birds, but birds and dogs leave each other alone otherwise.

The outdoor cages for the rest of the farm's adult parrots are arranged in rows that cover more than two acres. They are on metal stilts, so that the birds are at Cheryl's eye level as she and a visitor walk out to inspect them. A handsome Doberman bounds up to meet her. He is trained to guard this particular area and to kill the rats that would try to steal food from the cages at night. Other Dobermans guard other areas and patrol the high fence that surrounds the farm. The Forkers' parrots are well protected from anyone who might want to steal these valuable birds.

Some of the cages have a large population. One is full of small green parakeets that are about to be shipped by air to a pet shop. Other

*Some of the outdoor cages
at the Forkers' Florida parrot farm*
PHOTO BY SAM EPSTEIN

cages house only one bird. Cheryl gives a red-and-green parrot a treat from her pocket, and lets it press its beak against her mouth, in a kiss of greeting. She stops to speak fondly to a big white cockatoo which was one of the Forkers' original thirteen pets.

Most of the cages are home to a pair of birds.

"Look at these two!" Cheryl says, smiling at one pair. "They're so in love!"

In the next cage, only the male parrot can be seen.

"The female must be nesting," Cheryl says. "In there," she explains, pointing to a small box built into the rear wall of the cage, with an entrance big enough for only a bird to squeeze through.

She goes around to the rear of the cage and opens a little door into the box. Careful not to upset the mother, she counts the eggs she feels there. Later, back in the nursery, she will make a note of the number of eggs, along with the date, and will watch that cage with special care from now on. As soon as the eggs hatch, the new chicks will be moved to the nursery.

Everywhere, in row after row of cages, there are brilliantly colored birds. There are yellow-and-blue parrots. There are parrots whose greenish feathers are splashed with bright red. Cheryl picks up any feathers that have drifted to the ground. She will send them to Hopi Indian artists who use them to create traditional feather paintings and other works of art.

Cheryl explains why many parrots are now so rare. Once, they could be caught legally and were sold by the thousands. Also, many of the great tropical forests where parrots once lived have been cut down and replaced by farms, factories, towns, and roads.

Governments and bird lovers all over the world are now trying to increase the numbers of such rare birds. In some countries, it is against the law to catch certain wild parrots. People like the Forkers help by raising and breeding parrots which are growing more and more scarce in the wild.

One of the half dozen or more very rare birds that Cheryl raises is Buffon's macaw. This handsome yellowish-green bird, a native of Central America, has a small red patch above its big curved beak. There are pale blue feathers low on its back, and it has tail feathers of brownish red and olive yellow.

Cheryl points him out proudly, but she speaks with great concern when she says, "If we don't keep endangered birds like this alive, they will completely disappear from the earth."

Cheryl Forker is often invited to visit schools to show children how to look after pet birds. She takes several young parrots with her, and the equipment she uses to feed them. She says most children learn very quickly that cleanliness and a good diet are very important in the care of birds.

Sometimes one chick refuses to swallow the food she puts into its throat. Instead of letting the food settle down into its crop, the chick throws it up into Cheryl's hand. The children may be upset when that happens, but Cheryl is delighted, and tells the children why.

The thick liquid she feeds a chick, she says, makes a heavy lump in its crop. And so long as a bird's crop is heavy, it can't fly. Grownup birds, who eat seeds and other light foods, don't have heavy lumps in their crops, and that's one of the reasons they can fly. A chick that throws up its food, Cheryl says, is telling her that it no longer wants what she has been feeding it. It is saying that it is now ready to eat seeds—and fly!

"This chick is taking its first step toward growing up," Cheryl says.

She doesn't have to tell children that she hopes they will respect birds. They learn that lesson just by watching Cheryl Forker, who respects every bird on her parrot farm, and other birds of all kinds everywhere in the world.

CATFISH

Once the Fish No One Wanted to Eat

If you looked down from a plane flying over the flat part of Mississippi called the Delta—the Mississippi River flows beside it—you'd see what looks like long rows of large swimming pools. They are swimming pools, but for fish, not for people. The smallest of them is about three times the size of a football field. The largest pools are the size of thirty football fields put together. In these hundreds of pools, farmers raise the millions of catfish they sell to fish-loving customers every year, and the Delta is known as catfish country.

If you had flown over that part of Mississippi in the 1950s, you wouldn't have seen a single row of pools. You would have seen almost nothing but cotton fields. Then, and for more than a century before, the Delta was famous as cotton country, and its only catfish lived in rivers and streams. Many people didn't even bother to catch those fish, because, they said, catfish had a muddy taste and smell. Nobody ate catfish, they said, unless they couldn't afford to buy something better.

In the 1950s, though, new fabrics such as rayon and nylon were taking the place of cotton in clothes and other products. And Delta farmers, who were receiving lower and lower prices for the cotton they grew, were seeking new ways to earn money from their land.

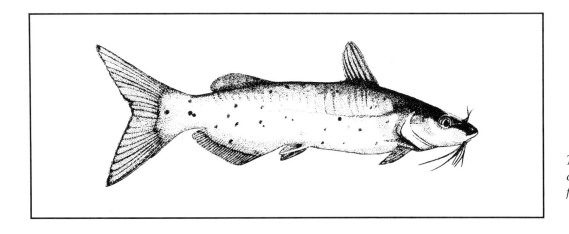

The cat-like whiskers on a catfish's lower lip give this fish its name
DRAWING COURTESY
DELTA PRIDE, INC.

Some of them thought of raising catfish to supply the newly popular sports clubs, where people paid a fee for the fun and sport of catching fish in the clubs' ponds. Those farmers dug ponds of their own, caught catfish to put in them, and when the fish had grown and multiplied, they were sold to the clubs. It wasn't a large market, but it was better than nothing.

Catfish are bottom feeders. They live on the dead fish, worms, and other creatures and decayed material they find on the muddy bottoms of their homes. The new catfish farmers began to wonder if the fish might not smell and taste better if they had a different diet. If the fish didn't taste and smell so muddy, the farmers thought, people might even be willing to buy catfish to eat. If that happened, catfish farming might become almost as profitable as cotton farming had once been.

A group of Mississippi farmers explored that possibility. Scientists of the United States Department of Agriculture agreed to help them. Together they developed catfish food in the form of pellets so light they floated on the top of the farmers' ponds. The catfish came up to the surface to feed on them.

The farmers' guess had proved correct. Top-feeding catfish, eating good food, no longer had a muddy taste and smell. People who refused to touch catfish caught in the wild were surprised at how much they liked the farm-raised fish. Markets and fish shops were soon willing to sell them. More farmers turned their cotton fields into rows of the huge catfish ponds that can now be seen from the air.

Catfish farming had become big business. At the same time, catfish-processing plants were being built. These plants bought the farmers' fish, skinned them, cut them up, wrapped them in neat packages, and shipped them in refrigerated trucks.

One small group of Delta catfish farmers decided it would be more profitable, and would also give needed jobs to their neighbors, to have their own processing plant. Other farmers agreed. So they formed a cooperative—a company they owned together—and in 1981 its 119 members built a plant in the small Mississippi town of Indianola. By 1989, the cooperative had three big plants in operation and was plan-

In ponds like these, Delta Pride farmers have raised over 100,000,000 pounds of catfish a year
PHOTO COURTESY
DELTA PRIDE, INC.

Catfish

ning a fourth. Delta Pride, as the farmers called their company, had become the largest processor of fresh fish in the United States.

"We all grew up together in this town, so we all know each other," explains the young woman who shows guests around the original Delta Pride plant. She is speaking of the workers in the plant, and of the company's owners. Among the owners are original members of the cooperative, who take an active part in its business while raising catfish in their own ponds.

Feeding nutritious floating pellets to his catfish is not all a Delta Pride farmer has to do to produce good-tasting fish. He must keep his ponds filled with clean water. And he must be sure the water has plenty of air in it, to give the fish the oxygen they need.

The water with which a farmer fills a pond comes from a deep well and is perfectly clean. But it won't remain clean very long once it becomes the home of thousands of catfish. Fresh clean water must be pumped into the pond constantly, while the stale, dirty water that settles toward the bottom of the pond flows out through a drainpipe. The fresh water also helps wash away the green scum that sometimes appears on a pond's surface. This scum is formed by microscopic plants called algae, which do not really harm catfish but can give them an unpleasant taste.

Oxygen is so necessary to fish—just as it is to human beings—that they die very quickly if they do not get enough of it. Farmers use machines called aerators to give the fish the steady supply of air that provides the needed oxygen. An aerator has large paddles attached to a shaft. As the shaft turns, the paddles beat the surface of the pond, splashing the water up into the air. There the drops of water absorb air and carry it with them as they fall back into the pond.

A catfish farmer tests the water in each of his ponds every few hours. If he finds one that does not have a good supply of oxygen, he moves extra aerators to it immediately.

The floating food pellets the farmers feed their catfish contain a healthy mixture of soybeans, corn, wheat, vitamins, and fish meal. The fish meal is made out of the bones, heads, and skin removed from the catfish in the processing plant. A small truck carrying a machine that looks rather like a cannon distributes the food. As the truck is driven along one side of the pond, the machine blows the food pellets out over the water.

Careful catfish breeding begins even before the fish are born. It starts in the spring, when a farmer selects from his ponds some of the male and female catfish that have been growing most rapidly. He knows they are likely to produce young that will also grow rapidly and be ready to market in the shortest possible time. He places the fish in a special breeding pond.

A catfish likes to lay her eggs in hidden places—under a rock, perhaps, if she lives in a stream. So the farmer puts large cans, each several feet tall, into this pond. The cans lie open, on their sides, on the pond bottom. Inside one of them a female lays her tiny eggs, stuck together in what looks like a lump of yellowish jelly. Then she swims away.

Her male partner, after fertilizing the eggs, takes up a position at the mouth of the can. There he remains, steadily swishing his tail back and forth. This motion forces fresh air-carrying water into the can and over the eggs. If the farmer didn't interfere, the male would stay at the mouth of the can for about seven days, until the eggs hatched.

But as soon as a farmer sees a male swishing his tail at the end of a can, he moves the eggs to a special hatching tank. There machines copy the male catfish's motion and keep water swirling around the eggs.

After the tiny catfish, called fry, are hatched, they are moved to one of the smaller ponds on the farm, where they will live for the next six months. At the end of that time, they will be five or six inches long. These fingerlings, as they are now known, are then transferred to the large pools which farmers call their grow-out ponds. They will remain there, growing steadily, from eighteen to twenty-four months—for as long as it takes them to reach a weight of about a pound and a half. At that weight, catfish are considered the best size for Delta Pride's markets.

When most of the catfish in a grow-out pond seem close to the right weight, the farmer scoops out a pair of them and takes them to the cooperative's fish taster. Only fish that meet this experienced taster's approval will be admitted to the processing plant and sold under the Delta Pride label.

The taster's test kitchen is a small room in the company's head-quarters, and his equipment consists of a knife, a fork, some brown paper bags, and a microwave oven. His test process is simple, and he repeats it all day long with each fish the farmers bring him.

First he cuts the fish in half, puts its meaty tail portion in a brown bag, and places the bag in the oven for a few minutes. When he takes the bag out, he rips it open and smells the steam coming from it. If the steam has a mild sweet odor, he goes on to the next step in the testing process.

Using his fork, he pulls off the surface of the fish so that he can reach the fatty section of flesh near the backbone. If that part of the fish has a pure-white color and a firm texture, he is finally ready to taste the fish. And only if its flavor is mild and sweet, with perhaps a little buttery or nutty taste, will the fish be given a final approval.

If the taster refuses to approve a farmer's pair of fish, the farmer knows there is something wrong with the pond he has taken them from. He must remove all the fish from that pond and clean it out. In the meantime, all the fish have been transferred to another pond. This is a long and difficult job. But if conditions in the second pond are just right, the fish will lose their poor smell or taste after several weeks. Samples of them will again be brought to the taster, and this time they may pass his severe tests.

If the farmer's fish win the taster's approval, the farmer knows that all the fish in the pond they came from are satisfactory. But the farmer must still have fish from that same pond tested again a week later,

Harvesting catfish is heavy work. A crane is used to lift this load of fish out of a pond

and then tested for a third time a week after that, on the day before he plans to harvest the fish from that pond. If the fish win the taster's approval all three times, harvesting begins the morning after the third test.

Tractors are stationed on both sides of the pond, which has a sloping bottom, so that one end of the pond is deeper than the other. A net is stretched between the tractors, and they move slowly along the length of the pond, beginning at the deeper end and forcing all the fish to move to the shallow end.

When all the fish are gathered there in a clump, workers unfasten the net from the tractors. They get into the water and raise the net's four corners out of the water to form a huge bag in which the fish are trapped. Fish too small to be accepted at the processing plant escape from the net, which has holes large enough for them to slip through. These fish will remain in the pond until they have reached the proper size for harvesting.

A truck carrying tanks filled with clean, constantly aerated water is waiting at that end of the pond. It is equipped with a crane for lifting heavy loads. The crane lowers a bucket-shaped net into the mass of trapped fish and picks up all the fish it can hold. That load is dropped into a tank on the truck, and the net is lowered again for a second load.

When all the truck's tanks are filled, it leaves immediately for the processing plant. But it will not be unloaded there until a sample of its cargo has passed one final test by the taster.

While a second truck is being loaded at the pond, the fish from the first truck are already being processed. They are first washed in clean water. Then their heads, skin, and insides are removed. Machines, or skilled workers, cut the fish into steaks, chunks, or fillets—a fish's whole boneless side. Finally, the fish are packed in large boxes for restaurants, or into small packages to be sold in stores and markets.

During the whole time the fish is being processed, it is kept cold to make sure it stays fresh. Some of it will be frozen before it leaves the plant. The rest of it will remain icy-fresh in the refrigerated trucks into which it is loaded.

The whole process takes very little time. While a catfish farmer is bringing a pond's last truckload to the plant, the first truckload may already be on its way to customers all over the country.

WEEDS

A Cause of Allergies
Makes a Cure

Travelers driving past the Sneed family's six-hundred-acre farm near the town of Sedalia, Missouri, often notice activities not common on a farm. They see people pulling handfuls of blossoms from trees and picking the flower heads off weeds. Or they see a huge machine that looks—and sounds—like a giant vacuum cleaner, moving slowly through a field of wheat or a patch of goldenrod.

What's going on? they may wonder. If they ask any of the Sneeds' neighbors, they get a quick answer. Everyone around Sedalia knows that the Sneed family collects pollen, the yellowish dust that all flowering plants produce.

"But why collect pollen?" is frequently the next question.

Another common query is: "Why would any farmer allow all those weeds to grow on his land?"

John Sneed can give a good answer to both questions. He could say that the Sneeds collect pollen, including the pollen of weeds, for some twenty million reasons. That's roughly the number of people in the United States who suffer, sometimes very seriously, if they breathe air containing one kind of pollen or another. When that happens, they may complain that they have hay fever. Doctors say they are suffering from an allergy.

If a man has an allergy to ragweed, for example, he may become ill each autumn. That's when he would breathe air in which tiny grains of ragweed pollen are floating. He wheezes and sneezes and coughs. His eyes water and his nose runs. He is miserable.

With the help of people like the Sneeds, however, he can avoid being so miserable. He can have repeated injections of a substance called an antiallergen. Its name tells us that it fights allergies. In this case, the antiallergen will be fighting the allergy caused by ragweed.

Each injection contains matter from ragweed pollen, but not enough of it to cause a serious attack of hay fever. There is enough, however, to make the sufferer's body start to build up a defense against ragweed pollen. As the man continues to get these injections, his body's

Goldenrod looks pretty to many people, but not to those allergic to this yellow-flowered weed
PHOTO BY SAM EPSTEIN

resistance to the pollen grows stronger and stronger. When the air is filled with ragweed pollen, his body's defense against it is strong enough so that he does not suffer the misery of a violent hay-fever attack.

Ragweed pollen has provided a kind of vaccination against the very allergy it can cause. And this is true of many other kinds of allergy-causing pollens. Weed harvesters like the Sneeds supply many of those valuable pollens.

John Sneed used to feel the way most farmers do about ragweed and all other weeds. He thought of them as pesky nuisances that could harm the crops he was raising—wheat, oats and other grains, hay for his Shorthorn cattle, and corn for his hogs. Then, one day in the late 1960s, a small group of men stopped at his farm. One of them asked if they might pick the ragweed they'd seen growing in a corner of the Sneed land.

He thought they must be joking. Pick weeds? He'd never heard of such a thing.

But they told him they were scientists from a laboratory in Oklahoma which needed the pollen of ragweed to make a ragweed-antiallergen. John Sneed told them they could pick as much ragweed as they wanted.

Not long afterward, he changed his own attitude toward weeds. The Oklahoma laboratory had offered to buy all the ragweed he could send them, cut and baled like hay. Any income he and his two sons could earn from a patch of weeds would be more than welcome, John Sneed thought. And weeds could be counted on to survive even the kind of bad weather that could destroy a crop of grain. From now on, he would think of weeds in a new way.

Simply harvesting and shipping ragweed didn't satisfy a man of John Sneed's curiosity for long. He learned that pollen from other kinds of weeds had value, too, and so did the pollen from trees, grains, and other grasses. Soon the Sneeds were shipping many varieties of plants and flowers.

The Oklahoma laboratory went out of business after a time, but by then the Sneeds were able to sell to some of the largest drug manufacturers in the country.

By then, too, John Sneed's curiosity had led him to make a study of how drug makers remove pollen from various plants and purify it for use in antiallergens. He decided the Sneeds could do that right there on their Sedalia farm, and ship out nothing but small packages of the yellow powder.

The manufacturers doubted that any farmer could carry out the delicate and difficult processes the Sneeds wanted to try. But one of them was so impressed by what John Sneed had already learned that its experts offered to show him and his family how to produce what the antiallergen maker needed.

Today the whole Sneed family works together in the business they call Ashland Farm Botanicals. John Sneed and his wife, Frances, own the company, and their daughter-in-law Stephanie handles correspondence and other business matters in the farm's office. Their son James is in charge of pollen collection. Their son Robert tends the crops and cattle that the farm has raised for generations. The grandchildren, Brian, Christen, and Jason, help, too.

The Sneeds sell pollen from twenty different kinds of trees, thirty varieties of weeds, and twenty grasses, including the oats, wheat, and other grains they've always grown.

The trees are those that have long stood on one part of the farm or another. The grains and other grasses have to be planted every year. The Sneeds plant some weeds, too. But they've discovered that weeds planted in rows, like their corn, don't grow as readily as those that spring up wild in open fields. So they usually just plow up certain fields and wait to see what happens. Almost any weeds that appear will yield a useful harvest of pollen.

The Sneeds couldn't possibly collect their farm's entire pollen production if it were all ready to be gathered at the same time. Fortunately, as John Sneed says, that doesn't happen. Each plant pollinates, or

James, Brian, and John Sneed preparing weeds for drying

PHOTO BY DAN WHITE
NEW YORK TIMES PICTURES

produces pollen, at the moment the tips of its tiny ball-shaped anthers open. These anthers, growing on thin stems in the center of a blossom, contain the yellow powder that is the flower's pollen. When the anthers open, the pollen puffs out. This happens at different times of the year for each type of plant on the Sneed land. Tree pollen, for example, appears in late February and early March, and grass pollen bursts out in May and June. The first weed pollen is produced in July, and other varieties follow, week after week, until the autumn frosts begin. Goldenrod pollen is usually the last weed pollen to be gathered.

Long experience has taught the Sneeds that the exact moment of pollination for each kind of tree, grass, and weed depends on weather conditions. "So you just have to sit there and be ready when they're ready," John Sneed says. "And if the bees are gathering around that same spot at the same time, you just have to be careful—but you'll still probably get some stings."

Some tree blossoms can be gathered by the handful. Other blossoms, like those of certain weeds, are picked one by one. And the

Weeds

collection of pollen from large fields of grasses or weeds is done by the giant vacuum cleaner the Sneeds put together out of parts of old farm machinery. Sitting on the vacuum cleaner's high seat, James Sneed drives it up and down the fields. As it travels, it sucks up the pollen from a ten-foot-wide strip of plants and blows the powder into a huge bag. This doesn't harm the plants, however, which means the Sneeds can later harvest their grain crops just as they did before those Oklahoma scientists asked if they might pick the farm's ragweed.

Pollen collection is the easiest part of the family's business, John Sneed says. The work that follows is more difficult, because all the pollen they collect is mixed with other material. The flower pollen is mixed with flower petals. The pollen sucked up by the vacuum machine

John Sneed running the "vacuum" that sucks up pollen. Brian follows, to pick up bags of pollen and carry them back to the barn

is mixed with bits of grass and stems and dust. All this material must be removed before purified pollen can be sent to a drug company.

The Sneeds use carefully worked out methods for purifying pollen. They spread the pollen-carrying blossoms and plants on racks to dry and then grind them into a coarse powder. That powder is then put through a sieve. Coarsely ground petals or stems remain in the sieve. The grains of pollen, so small they can be seen only through a microscope, fall through the sieve's tiny holes. But other unwanted material can fall through the sieve, too, so everything that has passed through the sieve will be sifted again, through finer sieves, until tests prove that it is at least 99.5 percent pure pollen. Then it can be packed and shipped to a drug manufacturer.

The Sneeds feel they are a lucky family. For one thing, their pollen business doesn't interfere with raising the crops and cattle the Sneeds have raised for generations and want to go on raising. For another thing, they all enjoy what they do.

And they're especially fortunate, they point out, because not one of them sneezes or wheezes or coughs in the presence of the pollen-producing plants they're near every day. Unlike the thousands of people who suffer from the allergies the Sneeds are helping to overcome, they themselves are not allergic to anything grown on their Missouri farm.

ALLIGATORS

A Source of Food and Leather

Every visitor to Florida's Gatorland, known as the Alligator Capital of the World, can see some five thousand alligators, and other animals as well. Visitors can even buy something made from an alligator. They might purchase an alligator-skin belt or purse or boots. They might have a lunch of alligator meat, or a bowl of alligator chowder.

This unusual farm—which didn't begin as a farm at all—belongs to the Godwin family. Godwins have lived in central Florida since shortly after the Civil War, when three Godwin brothers moved there from their Carolina home. In what was then a marshy and mostly empty region, they took up land grants being offered to war veterans. And on one of the dry areas called hammocks they began to raise cattle.

It wasn't an easy life. Florida cattle didn't grow very big or produce much beef. And the calves on the Godwins' Rattlesnake Hammock were menaced by alligators. But the Godwins kept their guns handy, and alligator skins were beginning to bring good prices from leather tanners.

In the 1920s, the Godwins were still raising cattle in central Florida, but that region was no longer as empty as it had once been. By then, automobiles were carrying Americans to every corner of the country, and thousands of them were coming to Florida to enjoy its warm, sunny winters. New roads and new hotels were built in central Florida, and along the coast, for the tourists. New towns were built for those who decided to stay.

Owen Godwin, of the third generation of Godwins in Florida, had been brought up to tend his father's herd, but as a young man he was always killing alligators, whether they threatened the cattle or not. He and his brothers paid to have the skins tanned, and their mother used the skins to make alligator-hide belts and purses to sell in her gift shop on the Godwins' land. Many of her tourist customers found the shop because they stopped to look at the little alligators Owen put in a roadside pond. He'd learned that Florida's newcomers were curious about the animal which had often been called "the ugliest creature that crawls or walks."

By the time Owen had gone to college, married, and was raising his four children, he owned a restaurant for tourists. But he was also beginning to think that what he really wanted to do was display Florida's alligators to its visitors in a proper setting—in a park-like zoo. He'd have snakes in his zoo, too, he thought; he'd made pets of them as a boy. And someday, he hoped, he would also exhibit animals from all over the world, so his neighbors could see foreign animals as strange to them as alligators were to people from Maine and Idaho.

As a first step toward realizing his ambitious plan, he sold his restaurant and bought fifteen acres of land, much of it marshy, near the town of Kissimmee. On it were two adjoining pits, known as "borrow" pits, common in the area. They had been dug by the state highway department to provide earth for the new roads it had been building through Florida's swamps. The story of earth "borrowed" from these pits should amuse the tourists, Godwin thought.

He connected the two pits, after his children had cleared them of weeds, to form one large hollow. Then he filled the hollow with water from a well, and built a bridge over the new lake he had created. He also built an office and a gift shop that looked like a stockade. The shop had a thatched palm-leaf roof, and sawdust on its floor.

Alligators, basking in the warm Florida sun, don't alarm their long-legged feathered neighbors

At first he put only thirteen alligators in his lake, but he brought another five hundred young ones to his property almost immediately. They moved sluggishly through the water. They sunned themselves beside it. They lay in the marshy areas, with almost nothing showing except their bulging eyes and the bony ridge behind them, called the scut. His snakes were housed in neat pens, and there was a sign outside the gate inviting the public to enter—free of charge!

Of course, Godwin hoped visitors would buy an alligator-skin belt or anything else that caught their fancy in his gift shop. And there was a box at the exit in which people were asked to leave as much money as they thought their visit had been worth.

People came. They looked. They listened when Owen Godwin told them that alligators were indeed known to have caught and eaten pet dogs and cats and even children. But his animals were well fed, he assured them, and wouldn't attack visitors who stayed behind the fences he'd erected. People seemed to enjoy his zoo and the animal stories he told. But at each day's end he found only a handful of pennies, nickels, and dimes in the box at the exit.

Then Owen added a thirteen-foot alligator to his collection. He'd bought Cannibal Jake, as he called the huge-jawed creature, from a woman whose son had owned it as a pet and then left it behind when he went off to school. She was eager to have the gator taken off her hands, and Godwin was eager to own it. He'd always believed that people like to look at animals they find frightening. Now he had a truly frightening one to show them.

Cannibal Jake was an instant success. And when summer arrived and the park's annual tourist season ended, Owen took the big alligator north in the special truck he'd designed for it. People could enter the truck and walk along the narrow passage, separated by heavy wire mesh from Cannibal Jake's cage. As they left the truck, a barrel awaited their contributions. After one trip north to New Jersey, the coins in the barrel added up to five thousand dollars.

As the years passed, Owen kept buying property, until his park was twice its original size. A fine new building replaced the first office and gift shop. A raised wooden walkway was built to lead visitors through the moss-draped cypress swamp where alligators still make their nests in the spring and lay their eggs. There were crocodiles, too, and snakes, of course, as there are to this day. Owen liked to pose for pictures with his thirteen-foot-long boa constrictor draped around his neck.

Before long, quite different kinds of animals were also brought in—deer, bears, a pair of zebras, ostriches, and monkeys. While his brother Charlie took Cannibal Jake north each summer, and as far west as California, Owen Godwin was making hunting trips to Alaska, India, and Africa. From each trip, he brought back exotic live creatures his neighbors had never seen. He liked to wear his safari jacket and his wide-brimmed hunter's hat with its snakeskin band when he told visitors where and how he had caught the zoo's new inhabitants.

The crowds at the park became too big to handle. For the first time a fee was charged to enter what had become known as Gatorland. There were other changes, too. As Gatorland's alligator population rose toward five thousand, Godwin was able to send some of the gators to other zoos. But by the early 1960s an alarm was out about the growing

*Many visitors are startled
by the Gatorland entrance*

scarcity of wild alligators. Too many of them were being killed, people were saying, by hunters eager to sell their valuable hides.

At about the same time, people were learning that the ancestors of alligators went back to the time of the dinosaur. And since alligators hadn't become extinct, as dinosaurs had, they seemed suddenly to have a special place in the animal world.

Laws were passed to halt the hunting of alligators. And although the laws were lifted after the alligator population was clearly no longer in danger, alligator hunting today requires a special license. The number of licenses issued is limited, and so is the number of alligators each hunter may take. Meantime, experts have been working to raise alligators in captivity, as the Godwins do, to make sure that these ancient creatures will never become extinct.

Today special care is taken at Gatorland as soon as the loud bellowing of the males, and their thrashing of the lake waters, announces the spring mating season. Members of the staff keep track of where each female goes when she enters the swamp to lay her eggs. Using her hind feet, a female pushes straw and leaves into a heap, makes a hollow at the top of the heap, and lays her eggs in that hollow. Usually there are about thirty-five eggs, but only part of that number will hatch in the sun's warmth while the female stands guard nearby.

But a female alligator is likely to wander far from her nest and perhaps never return. In that case, all the eggs may be eaten by snakes, herons, raccoons, or even by other alligators. So someone on the staff removes the eggs shortly after they are laid and takes them to the park's incubator room. The same thing is done if eggs are found in an abandoned nest in the wild. In the incubator room, the eggs will have the best possible chance to hatch into grunts, as the hatchlings are called. (The name comes from the grunting noise they make as they break through their shells.)

Eggs are removed from the nest very carefully. Before the first egg is lifted out, the top of each egg is marked, so that it can be kept in its original position. Turning an egg upside down might harm the alligator inside.

The temperature of the incubator room is kept at a very warm 88°F, and the humidity is high. The eggs hatch in about sixty-five days, and the new grunts are moved to a glass-walled nursery, where they remain for six months. There, on a diet of fish and meat high in protein, they grow to a length of about three feet. Alligators that are left to hatch in the wild grow only to about eight inches in that same period.

Two-month-old alligators. The one at the top was farm-raised

PHOTO COURTESY
GATORLAND

A skilled worker at Gatorland prepares to remove the very valuable skin of an alligator

PHOTO BY SAM EPSTEIN

At the end of two more years, spent in grow-out houses under carefully controlled temperatures, the young alligators are ready to join their elders in one of the park's several pools or in the big lake. There they will eat their share of the 150 tons of meat, fish, and chicken bought for the adult alligators every year. But by now they are about six feet long and may be slaughtered, or harvested, as the process is called, for their hides and meat.

By 1989, Gatorland was selling the meat and hides of a thousand alligators a year. Each one is given its own number before it is harvested and skinned. That number appears on the skin when it is sent to a tanner, and on every package of its meat sent out to stores and restaurants all over the country. This is done so that Florida government officials can check all alligator-meat sellers and users of alligator skins, to make sure that all products have come from an alligator that was legally raised and legally killed.

Members of the Godwin family, most of them still involved in Owen Godwin's park in one way or another, are proud of their farm and its products. Owen Godwin, who died in 1975, would almost certainly be proud of it, too, and would enjoy talking about it to the thousands of visitors who now pay their way into Gatorland each year.

RARE PLANTS AND ANIMALS

Making Sure These Heirlooms Aren't Lost

Don Shadow's plant nursery occupies part of the thousand acres of land he owns near the town of Winchester, Tennessee. There he grows ornamentals—the trees, shrubs, and flowering plants that people buy to ornament their yards and gardens.

Flowering plants and small bushes fill his hothouses. Larger bushes and trees stand in rows that stretch across his fields. His equipment is everywhere—plows, cultivators, tractors, and a tree-digging machine that can lift a tree right out of the ground, roots and all. In a large packing house, his customers' orders are prepared for shipping all over the country.

Like other nurserymen, Don Shadow tries to produce successful new varieties of plants by crossbreeding. If he crossbreeds two different kinds of rosebushes, for example, he hopes to produce a rose able to survive the diseases or severe weather that could kill its parents, or, perhaps, a rose more beautiful than either of its parents. Sometimes he succeeds. Some attempts fail. But failures don't discourage him. He goes right on trying to produce better plants. And in that way he is like other nurserymen.

But when an article about him appeared in *American Nurseryman*—

a magazine read by people in Don Shadow's business—it was called "Not Your Average Nurseryman." The title told readers what to expect. The author had visited Don Shadow, driven around with him in his pickup truck, and discovered just how different from the average nurseryman this one is.

Most nurserymen don't collect animals and birds. Don Shadow does. In fields, barns, and coops, he raises animals from every corner of the world. Some are wild animals. Others are the kind which farmers have long used to pull wagons or do other farm work, or which produce valuable wool, feathers, or skins, or which are slaughtered and sold as food. Domestic animals, they are all called—animals raised to be useful to human beings.

But some of Shadow's domestic animals are of a kind seldom used today, which means that very few people are raising them. And to Don Shadow—and a few other collectors, and some zoos, too—that's a good reason for breeding them. He believes that animals once important to farming should not be allowed to grow so scarce that they may eventually die out completely. Just as many people try to prevent the disappearance of endangered wild species, he tries to keep these domestic animals from vanishing.

When a visitor climbs into Don Shadow's pickup truck, it's rather like starting on a journey around the world. The visitor will see animals from every corner of the earth—about 150 of them altogether, representing some twenty-five different species.

The first stop might be beside a field enclosed by a wire fence. In its far corner there is a group of very small sheep. They are mouflon sheep, the host explains, from the islands of Corsica and Sardinia in the Mediterranean.

A pair of fat black creatures in another field are Guinea hogs. The traditional story of how these hogs came to this country, Don Shadow says, is that slaves brought them from their African homeland.

Standing aloof in another fenced pasture are two camels. But if the truck is driven into the pasture and Don Shadow opens his window,

Guinea hogs greet a visitor. They are said to have been brought to America by African slaves

PHOTO BY SAM EPSTEIN

they may move toward it and one may even poke its huge head into the cab to be petted.

His ostriches aren't as friendly as his camels. But if visitors approach, one or two are likely to move toward them, as if to find out who they are. These largest of the world's living birds can grow to a height of more than seven feet, and to a weight of over two hundred pounds. The three other large birds on Shadow's property are all smaller than ostriches. But these three, the crested cassowaries and emus from Australia, and the South American rheas, can all face a grownup visitor eye-to-eye.

Big Watusi cattle hear the sound of the truck's motor as it nears their field. They watch as Don Shadow lifts an armful of hay out of the truck and drops it over the fence.

"Come on, girlies!" he calls out. "Come on!"

And they do. Their huge horns gleam in the sunlight as they trot heavily toward him and reach for the hay. These handsome natives of Central Africa seem perfectly at home in Tennessee.

So do the dwarf black goats from Nigeria, which graze and run and jump in Don Shadow's field as if they'd always lived there. Some of them have. There are little black kids who were born on his farm and are as friendly as puppies, gathering around his feet to have their heads scratched.

Almost everywhere the truck can be driven on Don Shadow's land, there are animals or birds to look at. There are antelopes and cranes from Africa, guanacos from South America, donkeys from Sicily. And there are the famous donkeys from France called Poitou asses.

Since there may be only sixty of these small shaggy-haired asses still alive, Don Shadow felt very fortunate when he was able to acquire three jacks, or males; one jennet, or female; and the jennet's colt, another jack. He bought them from a California veterinarian who was unable to keep them himself because his neighbors objected to their braying. Don Shadow doesn't mind their noisy ways. He is delighted that, in owning these five creatures, he owns one of the largest herds of Poitou asses in the world.

The Watusis' huge horns give these cattle a misleadingly fierce appearance
PHOTO BY SAM EPSTEIN

Don Shadow with one of his Poitou asses

Don Shadow also owns a mare of the rare French breed of horses called Poitevin Mulassiers, of which there may be only several hundred in existence. One reason he is specially pleased to own her is that the history of this horse is part of the history of his Poitou asses.

That history stretches back several hundred years, to a time when France was ruled by kings. French animal breeders of that time had discovered that if they crossbred a Mulassier mare with a Poitou jack, the animal born to that pair grew up to be an especially tall and powerful mule. When French kings, noblemen, and generals decided that these mules were fit to pull their coaches, the breeders who provided the mules determined to keep the noble customers for themselves. They made sure that other breeders couldn't easily obtain the parent animals needed to produce the remarkable mules. Poitou asses and Mulassier horses were not common even in those days. And after the French Revolution, when noblemen had to give up their castles and their coaches, the handsome mules disappeared, too. And so, before long, did the horses and asses that could produce them.

That's another reason why Don Shadow is so pleased to own a Mulassier horse, along with his herd of Poitou asses. His Poitou jack and his Mulassier mare have already produced one of those special mules. And he hopes to have more of them in the future, so he wants to acquire more of the parent animals needed for this crossbreeding.

Raising endangered species of domestic animals and birds is only part of Don Shadow's plan for preserving the old ways. He also grows ornamental plants which were first bred and offered for sale many years ago but which have since been largely forgotten. Plants that have beauty or charm or other special qualities should be handed down from grower to grower, he believes, as people hand down jewelry and other family heirlooms from one generation to the next.

In the Shadow Nursery catalogue, which lists the plants Don Shadow has for sale, there is a special section called Heirloom Shrubs. For each plant named in that section, the date is given when it was bred and first offered for sale. A variety of hibiscus called Rose of Sharon, for example, was introduced in 1790, not long after George Washington became the first American President.

Don Shadow hopes that customers who buy some of his Heirloom Shrubs will also respond to another unusual page in his catalogue. This one lists things *he* wants to buy. Among them are other heirloom varieties of shrubs and trees, old breeds of animals and birds, and antique farm tools and machinery.

He says he collects such things so that someday he can open his own version of an heirloom farm to the public. It won't be simply a museum of old farming equipment, animals, and plants. It will be a workplace where visitors can watch a farm being run as farms were run a century or more ago. He already has a name for this project. It will be called Shadows of the Past.